20TH CENTURY MUSIC

1900-20

NEW HORIZONS

20TH CENTURY MUSIC – 1900-20
was produced by

David West ⚇ **Children's Books**
7 Princeton Court
55 Felsham Road
London SW15 1AZ

Picture Research: Carrie Haines
Designer: Rob Shone
Editor: James Pickering

First published in Great Britain in 2001 by
Heinemann Library, Halley Court, Jordan Hill,
Oxford OX2 8EJ, a division of Reed Educational and
Professional Publishing Limited.

OXFORD MELBOURNE AUCKLAND
JOHANNESBURG BLANTYRE GABORONE
IBADAN PORTSMOUTH (NH) USA CHICAGO

05 04 03 02 01
10 9 8 7 6 5 4 3 2 1

ISBN 0 431 14210 6 (HB)
ISBN 0 431 14217 3 (PB)

British Library Cataloguing in Publication Data

Hayes, Malcolm
1900-20 : new horizons - (20th century music)
1. Music - 20th century - Juvenile literature
I. Title II. Nineteen hundred-twenty
780.9'04

Printed and bound in Italy

Front cover: Edward Elgar (main image),
Igor Stravinsky.

The dates in brackets after a person's name
give the years that he or she lived.

An explanation of difficult words can be
found in the glossary on page 30.

20TH CENTURY MUSIC

1900-20
NEW HORIZONS

Malcolm Hayes

Heinemann
LIBRARY

CONTENTS

*RUSSIANS
IN REVOLT
In February 1917, the
Tsar of Russia and the imperial
government were overthrown by a popular
revolution. In October, Lenin (on the steps
with cap and beard) and his Communist
Bolshevik Party seized power.*

OLD WORLDS AND NEW

In 1900, music was poised on the verge of a new age. Over the next 20 years, completely new ideas were to take hold, in terms of what classical music could actually sound like.

The works of Arnold Schoenberg and his followers in Vienna began to explore wild extremes of intensity and dissonance. This is where music first began to sound seriously 'modern'. The other exciting musical centre was Paris, where a sequence of ballet scores by a young Russian, Igor Stravinsky, announced another explosive musical revolution. When the First World War broke out in 1914, the stability of European life and culture was swept away for good, but the radical ideas remained.

Meanwhile, music's future course was already being foretold across the Atlantic, with the rise of jazz, blues and ragtime. The new world was offering a new vision of what music itself could be, and could do.

THE BIRTH OF THE GRAMOPHONE
The earliest, hand-cranked gramophones, such as this 'Graphophone', seemed excitingly high-tech at the time, and began a new age of home listening.

The Graphophone
Makes Home Happy.
GRAND PRIX, PARIS 1903.

The World's
Best Talking Machine.
You can afford one because prices range from 25/- to £32.
We can suit you because we have
Thirty-five Different Styles.
Every One is a Good One.
You are missing one of the greatest pleasures of modern life if you haven't one in your home.
Write for Price List 17 to—
Columbia Phonograph Co., Gen'l.
122, Oxford Street, London, W.

MUSIC IN THE TRENCHES
Even amid the mud and horror of the trenches of the First World War, music was not forgotten.

STRAVINSKY
Igor Stravinsky (1882–1971) grew up in the imperial Russian city of St Petersburg. The world around him was soon to change utterly.

BETWEEN CENTURIES

At the dawn of the 20th century, two great figures towered over the musical world of the Austro-Hungarian and German empires. Gustav Mahler (1860–1911) and Richard Strauss (1864–1949) were not only major composers, but also two of the finest conductors of their time.

RADICAL SYMPHONIST

Mahler's music, though very popular today, was much more controversial in his lifetime. 'A symphony should be like the world,' he once said. So his own symphonies enormously expanded the 19th-century idea of an orchestral work in four movements. Several use solo and choral voices, like his Eighth, the so-called *Symphony of a Thousand* because of the huge number of performers required (in fact only several hundred!). Mahler also drew on the sounds of the wider world around him – bird-calls, military fanfares, and Austrian country dances.

RICHARD STRAUSS: MODERNISM, THEN SECOND THOUGHTS

Richard Strauss (not related to the earlier composers, both called Johann Strauss) started out as bold modernist. Aged 24, he had made his name with the symphonic poem *Don Juan*, and was already world-famous when his one-act operas *Salome* and *Elektra* shocked audiences with their lurid plots and dissonant music. But Strauss then changed direction, preferring the much more traditional harmonic style of his full-length operas *Der Rosenkavalier* and *Ariadne auf Naxos*.

GUSTAV MAHLER
Besides his composing, Mahler was famous as a great conductor. He was an idealist with ferociously high musical standards, and wasn't afraid of making enemies.

REHEARSING AN OPERA
Hans Pfitzner is standing behin the conductor (top left).

DER ROSENKAVALIER

Richard Strauss felt that for his own music, the past was as important as the future. *Der Rosenkavalier* (The Bearer of the Rose) is a romantic comedy set in the aristocratic world of 18th-century Vienna. First performed in Dresden in 1911, it was an instant and huge success. The music uses Viennese waltzes to create a world of humour, intrigue, and nostalgia – as if the violent upheavals of *Salome* and *Elektra* had never happened.

Richard Strauss (seated, centre) with colleagues

FINDING LIFE IN THE OLD WAYS

Hans Pfitzner (1869–1949) and Erich Wolfgang Korngold (1897–1957) were both conservatives at heart. Pfitzner created a masterpiece in his opera *Palestrina*, about a 16th-century Italian composer staying true to his genius despite the political and religious pressures around him. Korngold, a sensationally gifted child prodigy, was 13 when he wrote his first ballet, *Der Schneemann* (The Snowman). Alexander von Zemlinsky (1871–1942), though a traditionally minded composer, was also interested in the modernist world being explored by Mahler, and he too was a very influential conductor.

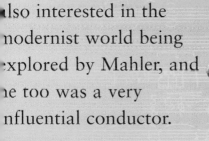

SALOME

Richard Strauss's opera, based on Oscar Wilde's play, was considered so shocking that it was banned or censored by the authorities in several cities.

FERRUCCIO BUSONI

At the turn of the century Busoni (1866–1924) was regarded as an important composer. He was also a magnificent pianist.

BREAKING WITH THE PAST

'Atonal' means 'not in any musical key'. This is still the usual description of the music that Arnold Schoenberg (1874–1951) found himself composing from 1908, rather to his own astonishment. Richard Wagner (1813–83) had lit a slow-burning fuse in his operas, whose intensity and complex chromatic harmony made them fiercely controversial works (which they still are). Fifty years on, the long-promised explosion now took place in the work of Schoenberg and his two most gifted pupils.

SCHOENBERG: THE RELUCTANT REVOLUTIONARY

Schoenberg was a gifted teacher of composition, who gave his pupils a thorough grounding in the musical styles of the past. His own music was so radical that he left tradition far behind. At the 1908 première of his Second String Quartet in Vienna, many people were appalled by its rootless, floating harmony. Others sensed the discovery of a thrilling new world.

VIENNA
At the beginning of the 20th century, Vienna was the capital city of the Austro-Hungarian Empire, with a great tradition of classical music which continues to this day.

COMRADES IN ARMS
Berg (left) and Webern were Schoenberg's two most talented pupils. Like their music, they were very different characters, but remained lifelong friends.

CITY LIFE
Vienna was an important trade and business centre, and its thriving musical life was built on this foundation of commercial strength.

8

IS MASTER'S VOICE (UP TO A POINT)

Anton von Webern (1883–1945) was a student and great admirer of Schoenberg, who took his example and developed it in his own direction. Webern's music from this period is extremely spare and concentrated. For instance, his Five Pieces for Orchestra (1911–13) together last for less than five minutes.

DIFFERENT FROM THE START

Alban Berg (1885–1935), another Schoenberg pupil, briefly and not very successfully tried to work in Webern's ultra-compressed style. His music changed when Schoenberg advised him to go back to tackling larger forms. The outcome was Berg's early masterpiece, the violent and darkly coloured Three Orchestral Pieces, which were written between 1914 and 1915.

PIERROT LUNAIRE

Pierrot Lunaire is a cycle of 21 poems originally in French, exploring the disturbed mind of a moonstruck Italian clown. Using a German translation, Schoenberg set them for a singer or actress and five instrumental players. In doing so he invented the new technical device of *Sprechstimme* (literally, spoken musical voice). This searches out the indistinct boundary between singing and normal speech.

Schoenberg, a master-composer

THE VIENNA COURT OPERA HOUSE

The Viennese people were (and are) passionate about opera. What happened there made newspaper headlines, and still does.

PARIS: IMPRESSIONISM AND SYMBOLISM

At the start of the new century, artistic life in Paris was the most colourful and varied in Europe. Painters, writers and composers were shaking off the academic restrictions of the past, while the city's freewheeling atmosphere attracted talent from other countries, notably the Ballets Russes company of the impresario Sergei Diaghilev.

EXOTIC APPEAL
A costume design for the Ballets Russes, the hottest ticket in town.

THE PROUD FATHER: CLAUDE DEBUSSY
Debussy was very fond of his daughter Claude-Emma, nicknamed Chou-Chou. In 1908, he completed Children's Corner, *six piano pieces that he dedicated to her.*

TWO QUIET REBELS
Debussy (right) believed passionately that music needed to be freed from the chains (as he saw them) of academic tradition. In this he found common ground with Erik Satie (left), whose simple but subtle compositions puzzled many concert-goers expecting something far more spectacular.

10

DEBUSSY: POET OF MYSTERY

The music of Claude Debussy (1862–1918) launched a quiet but bold revolution. 'In the opera house, they sing too much,' he said. So his only completed opera *Pelléas et Mélisande* (1893–1902) introduced a quite new style of composing for the stage – vivid, atmospheric and understated. In orchestral masterworks like *La Mer* (The Sea, 1905) and *Images* (1912), and also in his piano music, Debussy explored further his flair for supple rhythms and shades of instrumental colouring.

RAVEL: A MASTER OF THE ORCHESTRA

Maurice Ravel (1875–1937) liked to conjure exotic sounds and ancient worlds within more sharply defined structures than Debussy, and his piano works especially are more brilliant and spectacular. His masterpiece, the ballet *Daphnis et Chloé*, set in Ancient Greece, was premièred by the Ballets Russes in 1912.

VISITORS FROM THE SOUTH

Composers from all over Europe were drawn by Paris's cosmopolitan appeal. Two Spaniards, Isaac Albéniz (1860–1909) and Manuel de Falla (1876–1946), wrote some of their finest works there (Albéniz's 12-movement cycle *Ibéria* is one of the masterpieces of Spanish piano music). Gabriel Fauré (1845–1924) was composing some of his loveliest late works. Erik Satie (1866–1925) reacted to criticism of his piano pieces ('They're shapeless,' said a reviewer) by composing more, like his *Three Pieces in the Shape of a Pear*.

FAURE ENTERTAINS
Fauré was greatly respected by younger composers. Here, he is playing the piano at his home in Paris. On the left (with cigar) is his friend Albéniz.

11

ART IN PARIS
Paris was an exciting focus of developments in all the arts. The 'Impressionist' paintings of Claude Monet (1840–1926) have often been seen as the visual counterpart to the muted, half-toned atmosphere of Debussy's music. But Debussy himself preferred the work of other, different painters. He described the American James Whistler (1834–1903) as 'the greatest creator of mysterious effects in art'.

Whistler's Nocturne, blue and silver: Chelsea

FOLK SONG IN EUROPE

Much of central Europe, including what are now Hungary, Slovakia and the Czech Republic, was at this time part of the Austro-Hungarian Empire, ruled over by the Habsburg dynasty of Franz Joseph I in Vienna. Political nationalism had been growing throughout the Empire for many decades. Composers now began to reflect this in their music.

THE PEOPLE SING AND DANCE

The earliest works of Hungary's Béla Bartók (1881–1945) were influenced by the German concert-hall tradition of Richard Strauss. Bartók's discovery of Hungarian and Transylvanian folk music then brought about a radical change as he set about the task of cross-fertilizing these two different musical worlds within his own musical style, using dissonant harmony and driving dance-rhythms.

12

BRNO, CAPITAL OF MORAVIA
In the background (with the spire) is the Augustinian monastery, where the 11-year-old Janáček was sent to sing as a choirboy.

BARTOK AND KODALY
Bartók (seated left) and Kodály (far right) shared common musical ground in their commitment to the cause of the Hungarian people, although their own composing styles were rather different: Bartók was an instinctive modernist, Kodály more the tuneful traditionalist.

DISCONTENT IN HUNGARY
Budapest was Hungary's capital city. There, as throughout the Hungarian-speaking parts of the Habsburg Empire, political and cultural control remained mostly with German speakers appointed by Vienna. Kodály and Bartók were among those who wanted this to change.

A brilliant composer-pianist, Bartók also wrote impressively for the stage in his opera *Bluebeard's Castle* (1911) and ballets *The Wooden Prince* (1914–16) and *The Miraculous Mandarin* (1918–19).

THE COMPOSER AS TEACHER

Zoltán Kodály (1882–1967) worked together with Bartók on their travels to collect and write down the folk music they heard. The experience also influenced Kodály's own more relaxed and pictorial style. A gifted teacher, he started up a tradition of choral singing in Hungarian schools (it still thrives today) and wrote much music for it.

FROM SPEECH TO SONG

Born in the Czech region of Moravia, Leos Janáček (1854–1928) was another folk music collector. He also went further, sketching down in musical terms the everyday phrases that he heard spoken around him in the streets of the city of Brno and the Moravian countryside. 'I am trying to come close to the heart of humble Czech people,' he said. The result was a concise, vivid style of vocal writing which first flowered in his great opera *Jenufa* (1894–1903).

13

ROMANY MUSICIANS

In the early 20th century, central Europe was still a largely rural world of poverty-entrapped villages and small towns. The mass movement of populations towards the cities and hoped-for prosperity had already begun. But while the countryside's folk music tradition was dying out, Bartók and Kodály found much of it still surviving, kept alive especially by the travelling Romany people.

Travelling folk musicians of eastern Europe

RUSSIA: REVERIE AND REVOLUTION

Imperial Russia under Tsar Nicholas II was a backward-looking, authoritarian world, whose government was finding it increasingly difficult to suppress popular demands for political change. In the same way, Russia's composers found themselves divided into those who needed no other world than the one they knew, and others who saw themselves as angry radicals.

PROKOFIEV: THE YOUNG REBEL

Serge Prokofiev (1891–1953) upset his teachers at the St Petersburg Conservatory with his early, aggressively rhythmic works and the extravagant style of his Second Piano Concerto (1913). A springer of surprises, he also came up with his wry and engaging First Symphony (the 'Classical', 1918). Prokofiev decided to leave post-Revolutionary Russia for a new life in the USA in 1918.

ALEXANDER SCRIABIN
Scriabin, too, was a remarkable pianist. As a child, he practised so hard that one of his piano's pedals wore through the sole of his shoe.

14

PROKOFIEV THE FIREBRAND
Prokofiev was a brilliant pianist. While he was still a student, he amazed his contemporaries by composing and playing works that pushed back the boundaries of piano technique.

A LATE, GREAT ROMANTIC

The success of his Second Piano Concerto in 1901 launched Sergei Rachmaninov (1873–1943) on a triple career as a composer, conductor, and one of the century's great pianists. His music, at once passionate and melancholic, remained true to the tradition and spirit of Russian Romanticism. Rachmaninov felt that there was no place for himself or his family in post-Revolutionary Russia. He took his family with him on a tour of the Nordic countries in 1918. Later that year, they arrived in New York, to settle eventually in the USA.

Revolution brews in Imperial Russia.

A TRUE ALL-ROUNDER

Rachmaninov was music director of the Bolshoi Opera in 1904–06. Standing behind him here are two singers in the cast of his opera Francesca da Rimini (1906).

A COMPOSER WHO TOOK HIMSELF SERIOUSLY

Pre-Revolutionary Russia was full of strange, semi-religious cults. The composer-pianist Alexander Scriabin (1872–1915) thought of himself as a Messiah figure for future music. He wanted to build a temple in India and perform in it his *Final Mystery* for piano, massed choirs, orchestra, and an imaginary form of light-projection. Only sketches for the project survive. What might it have sounded like? Scriabin's *The Poem of Ecstasy* (1908), with its shimmering orchestration, gives an idea.

EXOTIC DREAMS

Léon Bakst was the Ballets Russes' acclaimed designer. This is one of his designs for a ballet based on Scheherazade by Nikolai Rimsky-Korsakov (1844–1908), a masterpiece from 'Old' Russia.

15

ITALY: PUCCINI AND OPERA

In Italy, opera was everything – well, almost. When the great Giuseppe Verdi (1813–1901) died, his status as the uncrowned king of Italian opera passed to Giacomo Puccini (1858–1924). Meanwhile, other composers were looking for ways of steering Italian music towards a new future.

Tragic heroine

MASCAGNI FINDS IT TOUGH AT THE TOP

Pietro Mascagni (1863–1945) claimed to be the composer who launched *verismo* (see p. 17) single-handed with *Cavalleria Rusticana* (Rustic Chivalry, 1889), his one-act opera about Sicilian peasant life. But world fame did not help him to achieve another success on anything like that scale, although his *Isabeau* (1911) and *Lodoletta* (1917) are sometimes performed today. He and Puccini once shared lodgings together, but Mascagni later became jealous of his star rival. Ruggiero Leoncavallo (1857–1919), too, never quite repeated the success of *Pagliacci* (Clowns, 1892), although his comedy *Zazà* (1900) came close.

MASCAGNI
Cavalleria Rusticana *made the almost unknown Mascagni famous overnight.*

COLLEAGUES AND RIVALS
Mascagni (left) and Puccini (right), with the composer Alberto Franchetti (1806–1942) at the piano. Puccini's career began much less successfully than Mascagni's, but he soon learned brilliantly from his mistakes.

16

MADAM BUTTERFLY

'Puccini's flop,' said the newspaper headlines in Milan on 18 February 1904. The night before, *Madam Butterfly* had been greeted with silence by the audience in the city's La Scala opera house. Puccini set about revising his opera about a Japanese girl who is abandoned by her American naval-officer husband, and kills herself in despair. The new version was premièred three months later, and has been one of 'Puccini's Greatest Hits' ever since.

A CRUEL STORY
Puccini's Tosca is set in 19th-century Rome. Here the heroine, Floria Tosca, watches her lover Cavaradossi (right), a political prisoner, go through what they both believe to be a mock execution by firing squad. But the bullets are real.

PUCCINI
In 1910, Puccini completed La Fanciulla del West (The Girl of the Golden West) for New York's Metropolitan Opera House.

SHOCK, HORROR – AND THE PUBLIC LOVES IT

The late 19th century had seen the rise of the *verismo* ('reality') movement in opera. Its followers insisted that traditional grand opera had had its day: down-to-earth, sordid stories, they said, deserved a place on the operatic stage. Puccini seized on the idea in his wildly successful *Tosca* (1900), where the heroine murders the villain after listening to the screams of her lover being tortured by his henchmen off stage.

BACK TO THE FUTURE

Gian Francesco Malipiero (1882–1973) was an expert in his country's rich heritage of music from previous centuries, especially the works of Claudio Monteverdi (1567–1643). This music inspired Malipiero to blend its sharply focused style of expression with modern European developments in his own compositions. Another who looked beyond Italy was Alfredo Casella (1883–1947), who was influenced by Richard Strauss and Mahler, and later by Stravinsky and Bartók.

NORDIC SYMPHONIES

Musical life in the northern European countries had always trailed behind the great powerhouses of Germany, Austria, Italy and France. Finland did not even have a symphony orchestra until 1884. Yet this small, remote country produced one of the century's greatest composers, Sibelius, and nearby Denmark gave the world Carl Nielsen.

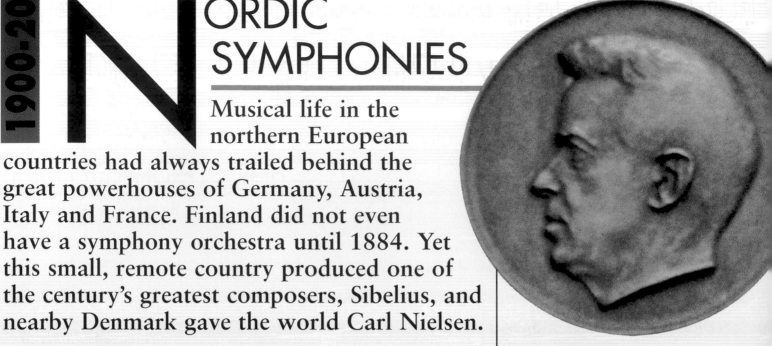

CARL NIELSEN
Nielsen came from a poor background on the Danish island of Odense, where his father taught him to play the violin and the piano.

A MIGHTY VOICE FROM THE NORTH

As a young student in Helsinki, Finland, Johan Sibelius (1865–1957) dreamed of becoming a violin virtuoso. When this didn't work out, he went to study composition in Berlin and Vienna. (He later changed his name to 'Jean', in upmarket French style.) Returning to Finland, which was then part of the Russian empire, Sibelius became involved in the Finnish nationalist movement for independence. Finnish folk poetry and stories inspired his early works.

SIBELIUS WITH BUSONI
Ferruccio Busoni (left), the German-Italian composer pianist, and Sibelius were old friends. In his memoir the English conductor Sir Henry Wood recalled: 'I never knew where they would get to... They were lik a couple of irresponsible schoolboys.'

arly successes soon made Sibelius a national
ero – the tune of his symphonic poem *Finlandia*
1900), originally entitled 'Finland Awakes!',
ecame his country's unofficial national anthem.
le found fame abroad, mostly in Britain and
merica, with his cycle of seven symphonies.

YMPHONIES WITH A DIFFERENCE

arl Nielsen (1865–1931) first earned his
ving as an orchestral violinist, and played
n the première of his First Symphony in
892. He became an important composer
nd teacher, also composing operas for the Royal Danish
heatre in Copenhagen: his comic opera *Maskarade* (1906) is
egarded as Denmark's national masterpiece. Nielsen developed the
nusual idea of 'progressive tonality', where a symphony travels
owards an ending in a different musical key from which it began.
lis Fourth Symphony (1916) is subtitled 'The Inextinguishable'.
Music is life,' Nielsen once explained. 'Like life, it cannot
e extinguished.'

19

The 'Land of a Thousand Lakes'

MUSIC AND NATURE
For Sibelius, music and the Finnish
landscape went together. He was
able to build large musical
structures out of repeated,
endlessly developed
fragments of melody – an
idea which grew partly
from his research into
Finnish folk singing. The
result was a spare, but
highly effective technique
of composing, capable
of great power, and
often suggesting the
vast empty spaces of
the snowbound
Finnish countryside.

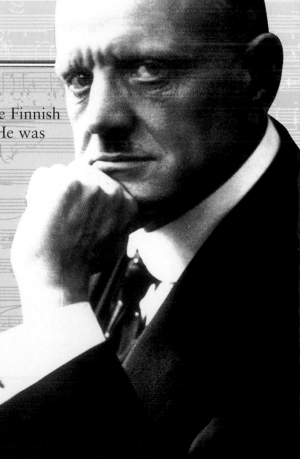

A NEW MUSIC: RAGTIME

Blues was the original music of America's black population. It emerged from the cotton plantations of the Deep South, and made its way north to the big cities. Jazz made a similar journey, spreading out from its roots in New Orleans to conquer the world. Both were about to have a huge influence on classical music, in America and beyond.

I GOT THE BLUES

Blues allowed musicians to improvise against the fixed shapes and rhythms of verses. It flourished in vaudeville, the South's style of music-hall entertainment, and produced great singers in 'Ma' Rainey (1886–1939), Bessie Smith (1895–1937), and the unrelated Clara Smith (1894–1935).

AHEAD OF HIS TIME
Scott Joplin is known to have heard a recording of the overture to Wagner's opera Tannhäuser. But he was barred from hearing enough classical music to develop his composing technique, as he so wanted to.

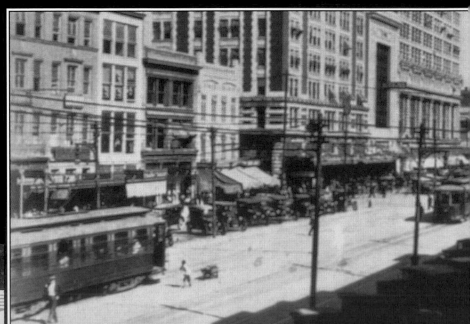

BESSIE SMITH
At first a member of 'Ma' Rainey's vaudeville troupe, the Rabbit Foot Minstrels, Bessie Smith soon became one of the biggest blues stars in her own right, with her powerful delivery and brilliant way of timing a phrase. She died tragically in a road accident.

20

A SOPHISTICATED ENTERTAINER

Ragtime was usually piano music, where the right hand played in 'ragged time' against the regular rhythmic patterns of the left (a technique known as syncopation). In Scott Joplin (1868–1917), it produced the gifted composer of *Maple Leaf Rag* and *The Entertainer*. Joplin also wrote two operas, *A Guest of Honor* (1903) and *Treemonisha* (1911), but his ambitions were thwarted by discrimination: black people were not then allowed to enter an opera house.

JAZZ SWEEPS AMERICA

The roots of jazz overlapped with those of blues and ragtime. It was played as much as sung, in bands with the trumpet, trombone and clarinet as improvising soloists and a rhythm section of guitar or banjo, drums, string bass and piano.

THE GREAT AMERICAN MUSICAL

The 'musical' had now grown from operetta and variety shows into a mix of song, story and dance. On New York's Broadway, George M. Cohan (1878–1942) wrote and directed a string of hits including *Little Johnny Jones* (1904) and *The Honeymooners* (1907). Irish-born Victor Herbert (1859–1924) wrote the songs for *Babes in Toyland* (1903), *Naughty Marietta* (1910) and others. Irving Berlin (1888–1989) became famous with his song 'Alexander's Ragtime Band' (1911) and the shows *Watch Your Step* (1914) and *Stop! Look! Listen!* (1915).

'MA' RAINEY

Born Gertrude Pridgett in Columbus, Georgia, 'Ma' Rainey took her name from her husband, vaudeville dancer William 'Pa' Rainey. She was known as 'the mother of the blues'.

NEW ORLEANS

While blues originated in the cotton-growing country of the South, jazz has always been urban music. Its home was New Orleans, the colourful city in the state of Louisiana on the delta of the Mississippi River.

TUXEDO BAND

When the original Tuxedo Band made early recordings of jazz in 1917, the music had already travelled a long way from its origins among black Americans in the South. The Band made its name playing in New York City, and produced several musicians who went on to be jazz stars in their own right, such as Clarence Williams. Jazz was now the favourite entertainment of rich, white audiences as well as poor, black ones.

The Tuxedo Band, with Clarence Williams (bottom)

AMERICA: FROM ROMANTICISM TO IVES

Classical music in America at this time was an imported, 19th-century European product for prosperous, middle-class communities in the towns and cities. Against this conventional background, the wild originality of Charles Ives (1874–1954) came like a bolt from the blue.

EUROPEAN EXAMPLE
George W. Chadwick studied in Germany and then returned to teach music at Boston's New England Conservatory.

EUROPEAN INHERITANCE

Edward MacDowell (1860–1908) went to study piano-playing and composing in France and Germany. He then returned home and composed, played, taught at Columbia University, and relaxed by conducting a men's glee club. He was a genuinely Romantic spirit, although his music does not sound particularly American. George Chadwick (1854–1931) and Arthur Foote (1853–1937) also composed successfully within the musical forms of the European classical tradition.

HOME-GROWN TALENT
Arthur Foote studied at Harvard University with the American composer John Knowles Paine (1839–1906) and then settled in Boston, where he became an admired composer, organist and teacher.

A WOMAN COMPOSER BEFORE HER TIME

When Amy Beach (1867–1944) married at the age of 18, her husband asked her to cut down on her appearances as a brilliant concert pianist. Composing, he said, was a more suitable occupation for a married woman, and she adapted to this new life. She produced over 300 works under the name of Mrs H.H.A. Beach.

AMY BEACH

'No other life than that of a musician could ever have been possible for me,' wrote Amy Beach. Even so, it took all her determination to succeed in a man's world. It was only after her husband died, in 1910, that she was able to start touring Europe as a concert pianist. Her strongest music has real passion, although it still speaks with a European accent.

A true pioneer among composers

BROADWAY, NEW YORK IN 1912
Ives even tried portraying the activity of city crowds in music.

ADVENTURES IN SOUND

Ives's music explored advanced ideas like polytonality, where different sections of an orchestra play in different keys at once, like different bands being overheard outdoors at the same time. In Central Park in the Dark (1906), orchestral sounds suggesting the quietness of the empty park itself are increasingly overlaid by noisy bursts of jazz-like music from a nearby café. These are played at the same time by a different orchestra in a different tempo, so that two conductors are needed. Nothing quite like this had ever been written down before.

IVES: A NEW ENGLAND MAVERICK

Charles Ives was American classical music's first genius. The son of a bandmaster in Danbury, Connecticut, Ives took in all the different sounds of the New England world around him – hymns, popular songs and bands, besides classical music itself. Ignoring every conventional rule, he assembled his musical ideas into tapestries of sound that can be astonishingly daring and dissonant. For instance, in 'Puttnam's Camp' in *Three Places in New England* (1908–14), the orchestra imitates several bands playing at once. Ives was a partner in an insurance business, which meant that he could compose only at weekends. His music sounded very modern for its time, and only began to be properly appreciated near the end of his life. His wildly complicated *The Fourth of July* (1913) was not heard for many years. *Three Places in New England* was only premièred in 1931.

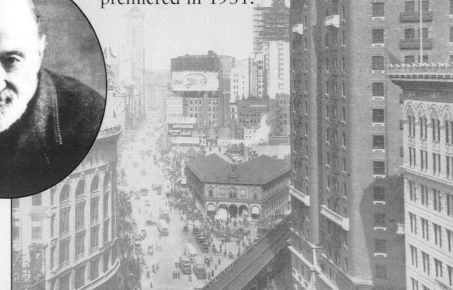

STRAVINSKY

No composer has ever leapt to fame from more unpromising beginnings than Igor Stravinsky (1882–1971). In 1909 he was an unknown former pupil of the traditionally minded Russian composer Nikolai Rimsky-Korsakov (1844–1908), who at first had not thought Stravinsky had much talent. Just four years later, Stravinsky had written three great ballet scores. Each of them unleashed a rhythmic firepower that changed western music for ever.

24

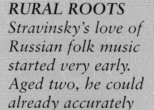

RURAL ROOTS
Stravinsky's love of Russian folk music started very early. Aged two, he could already accurately sing the folk songs he heard around him.

HOW TO MEET A DEADLINE

Stravinsky owed his breakthrough to Sergei Diaghilev (1872–1929), the Russian impresario who had founded the Ballets Russes company. In 1909, a commission for the company's next Paris season needed a composer at short notice. Diaghilev took a chance on Stravinsky, who worked at lightning speed and completed *The Firebird* in just five months. Based on a Russian folk tale, it was a sensational success. Stravinsky became famous overnight.

The ungainly appearance of Nijinsky's dancers was shocking.

PETRUSHKA: A PUPPET DANCES

Diaghilev wanted more 'hits', and Stravinsky provided them. In 1911, he composed the ballet *Petrushka*. Its daring use of bitonality (musical ideas in two different keys at once) broke new ground in western music.

The story is about the sad love-life of a puppet (perhaps he's also human?) in a fairground show in St Petersburg. Stravinsky portrays this world in disconnected blocks of orchestral sound, held together by the rhythmic energy that drives them along. The idea was quite new. Stravinsky then took it even further.

THE RIOT OF SPRING

The first performance of *The Rite of Spring* in 1913 started the most famous riot in musical history. By the standards of classical ballet, the story was X-rated: at an imaginary ceremony, a young girl dances herself to death. The audience was outraged by the music's pounding rhythms and extreme dissonance. But after a triumphant performance the next year, Stravinsky was carried shoulder-high along the Paris streets by a crowd of admirers.

AHEAD OF ITS TIME

The audience's fury at *The Rite of Spring's* première probably related more to Nijinsky's choreography than to Stravinsky's music. In classical ballet, gravity-defying lightness is emphasized, and the dancers' feet point outwards. This picture shows that Nijinsky had them doing the opposite, as he tried to convey the music's earth-stamping power in visual terms. He had begun to invent modern dance.

VASLAV NIJINSKY
Nijinsky (illustrated here by Georges Barbier in 1913) was the most gifted dancer of his day, and the Ballets Russes' biggest draw. He also had bold and experimental ambitions as a choreographer. His virtuoso performance in Petrushka's title role was the talk of Paris in the summer of 1911.

ENGLAND: SUNSET AND DAWN

At the start of the 20th century Britain had an empire on which, it was proudly said, 'the sun never sets'. But England's composers preferred to stand aside from this apparently secure and serene world (which was soon to be engulfed in mechanized war). Some reacted against it, and turned instead to their country's musical grass roots for ideas and inspiration.

POMP AND CIRCUMSTANCE (ON THE OUTSIDE ONLY)

The proud Empire itself seemed to speak through the most popular music of Edward Elgar (1857–1934), like his *Pomp and Circumstance Marches* (the tune of 'Land of Hope and Glory' comes from one of them). But the real Elgar is found in much larger and deeper works such as the oratorio *The Dream of Gerontius* (1900) and his two symphonies. They contain dark warnings of upheavals to come, alongside the inner strength that Elgar drew from his Catholic faith.

THE DREAM OF GERONTIUS
Elgar's oratorio is now one of his most loved works, but at its first performance, the choir and players found the music strange and difficult. The illustration above portrays the journey of Gerontius's soul after death towards the sight of God.

ELGAR IN THE STUDIO
Elgar was interested in gramophone recordings, and made some of the very earliest ones. The device in front of him funnelled the sound of the orchestra towards a microphone.

26

GO WEST, YOUNG MAN

The young Frederick Delius (1862–1934) was sent by his father to Florida to manage an orange grove. Delius's music was marked for life by the tropical glow of his surroundings and the sound of black male voices singing as they worked. Returning to Europe and living mostly in France, he produced two radiant masterworks in his opera *A Village Romeo and Juliet* (1901), a tragic story of young love, set in Switzerland, and his anti-religious oratorio *A Mass of Life* (1905).

A POET IN SOUND
Delius had strong links with the cultures of Germany and Scandinavia. The mountain landscapes of Norway inspired his A Song of the High Hills (1911) for wordless chorus and orchestra.

THE COUNTRYSIDE ENDURES

Aiming to renew the deepest values of English music, Ralph Vaughan Williams (1872–1958) went back to basics in a different way. He edited English hymn tunes, researched English music of earlier centuries, and collected folk songs in the English countryside. He combined all these influences in works like the *Fantasia on a Theme of Thomas Tallis* (1910) and *The Lark Ascending* (1914). *A Sea Symphony* (1909) is a choral setting of words by the American poet Walt Whitman.

THE PLANETS

Gustav Holst (1874–1934) and Vaughan Williams shared a common interest in the folk music they collected together. But Holst also had more exotic interests, like the astrological star-signs that inspired his orchestral suite *The Planets* (1914–17). Many believed that the battering rhythms of its opening movement, *Mars, the Bringer of War*, were a vision of the First World War, but Holst always denied this.

A postage stamp, commemorating Holst's most famous work

MASTERPIECES
Holst (left) also composed Savitri *(1908), a chamber opera on a Hindu story, and* The Hymn of Jesus *(1917) for chorus and orchestra.*

WAR DESTROYS THE OLD WORLD

The First World War broke out in August 1914. When it ended over four years later, Europe was a different place. The defeated German and Austro-Hungarian empires were broken up by Britain and France, the exhausted victors, while Russia descended into the chaos of revolution. The lives of composers were changed like everyone else's.

A GENIUS REGROUPS AND STARTS AGAIN

Stravinsky was marooned during the war in the neutral country of Switzerland. Wartime conditions meant that the lavish productions of the Ballets Russes were no longer possible. So Stravinsky struck out in a new direction, writing works for much smaller forces. He arranged Russian folk songs, and sketched out a Russian ballet *Les Noces* (The Wedding, 1914–17). *Renard* (The Fox, 1916) was a bolder idea: a story about farmyard animals, portrayed by singers and acrobats.

THE SOLDIER'S TALE

Working with the Swiss poet C.F. Ramuz, Stravinsky composed *The Soldier's Tale* (1918) for a travelling theatre group. The story – about a soldier who sells his soul to the devil as the price of love and riches – is portrayed by actors, a dancer, and a group of seven musicians. Out of the blue, Stravinsky had come up with the first example of what we now call music theatre.

Stravinsky (seated) visiting Debussy

CALLED UP
Schoenberg spent the war in and out of the Austrian army, although he was not sent to the front. Webern constantly petitioned the authorities to exempt Schoenberg from military duty, because of his former teacher's national importance as a composer.

LIFE AT THE FRONT
Pictures like this one (probably posed) suggested that in the First World War, the front line wasn't such a bad place to be. In reality the mechanized slaughter, poison gas and mud were a nightmare, from which Europe has perhaps never quite recovered.

STAIRWAY TO HEAVEN

Like his pupils Webern and Berg, Schoenberg was called up into the Austrian army. Between on-off periods of wartime service he set about composing *Die Jakobsleiter* (Jacob's Ladder, 1917). This was planned as a vast oratorio, about the meeting of heaven and Earth which the biblical figure of Jacob saw in a dream. Schoenberg never completed it, but even so, the unfinished oratorio is one of his greatest achievements.

DIFFERENT RESPONSES

When the war broke out, Ravel quickly completed one of his finest works, his Piano Trio (1914). He then joined up, driving a military ambulance at the Western Front, where the German army had invaded France. Increasingly ill with cancer, Debussy wrote a brilliant set of piano *Etudes* (Studies, 1915) before his death in 1918. Richard Strauss, living at his mountain home in German Bavaria, went on composing almost as if the war wasn't happening. In 1919 he completed his grandest opera, *Die Frau ohne Schatten* (The Woman without a Shadow).

SITTING IT OUT
Richard Strauss composed busily during the war years. Besides his work on the vast score of Die Frau ohne Schatten, *he wrote a chamber opera,* Ariadne auf Naxos (Ariadne on Naxos), *which was premièred in 1916.*

ON SERVICE
Ravel felt it his duty to serve his country during the war, although he had to stop composing for a time.

GLOSSARY

ATONALITY A term meaning 'music in no key', often describing the work of Schoenberg and his followers. Schoenberg preferred 'pantonality' (music in all keys at once).

CHROMATIC (from the Greek word *chromatikos*, 'coloured') Used to describe music whose different harmonies are more extreme than those of earlier composers, such as Mozart.

CONCERTO A work for solo instruments and orchestra.

DISSONANT (or 'discordant') Two or more notes which, when played together, produce a harsh, unstable sound.

GLEE CLUB An amateur group for singing unaccompanied songs in England and America.

IMPROVISED Music which is not written down, but composed at the moment it is performed.

KEY The bedrock idea of classical music, where the harmony sounds fixed to a particular 'keynote'.

MODERNISM A term which loosely describes music that sounds modern compared to earlier music.

ORATORIO A setting of a text on a religious subject, for solo voices, chorus and orchestra.

PIANO TRIO A work for a violin, cello and piano.

SOPRANO The highest type of female voice.

STRING QUARTET A work for four stringed instruments: two violins, viola and cello. Also the group that plays it.

SYMPHONIC POEM A work for orchestra, usually in a single movement (section), telling a story or depicting a particular scene (say in a city or the countryside). Sometimes referred to as a 'Tone poem' (a mistranslation of the German word *Tondichtung*, which means 'sound-poem').

SYMPHONY Traditionally, an orchestral work in four movements. By the 20th century this form could be much expanded to include several more movements, sometimes also using solo and choral voices. There are also one-movement symphonies.

WALTZ A swirling ballroom dance, in rhythmic units of three beats. Waltzes were much loved in Vienna.

WORLD EVENTS

- 'Boxer' Rebellion in China — 1
- First transatlantic radio transmission — 1
- Boer War ends in South Africa — 1
- First powered flight, by the Wright brothers — 1
- Start of Russo-Japanese War — 1
- First Revolution in Russia — 1
- San Francisco earthquake — 1
- Maiden voyage of the liner Lusitania — 1
- Henry Ford launches the Model T motor car — 1
- Blériot is the first to fly from England to France — 1
- Japan annexes Korea — 1
- Chinese Revolution deposes the Emperor — 1
- The liner Titanic sinks — 1
- Henry Ford invents the assembly line — 1
- First World War breaks out — 1
- ANZAC defeat at Gallipoli, Turkey — 1
- Easter Rising in Dublin — 1
- Russian Revolutions in February and October — 1
- End of First World War — 1
- Treaty of Versailles — 1

TIMELINE

	MUSICAL EVENTS	THE ARTS	FAMOUS MUSICIANS	MUSICAL WORKS
0	•Première of Leoncavallo's Zazà	•Death of Oscar Wilde, Irish writer	•Birth of Aaron Copland, American composer	•Mahler's Fourth Symphony
1	•Rachmaninov plays Second Piano Concerto	•Buddenbrooks, first novel by Thomas Mann	•Birth of Jascha Heifetz, American violinist	•Elgar's Pomp and Circumstance March No. 1
2	•First recordings by Enrico Caruso	•Heart of Darkness, novella by Joseph Conrad	•Birth of jazz clarinettist Omer Simeon	•Pélleas et Mélisande, opera by Debussy
3	•Janáček completes his third opera, Jenufa	•Call of the Wild by novelist Jack London	•Birth of jazz drummer Ben Pollack	•Pelleas und Melisande, this time by Schoenberg
4	•Puccini's Madam Butterfly flops in Milan	•Chekhov's The Cherry Orchard first staged	•Birth of Coleman Hawkins, jazz saxophonist	•Debussy's L'Isle Joyeuse for piano
5	•Lehár's operetta The Merry Widow premièred	•Exhibition of 'Fauvist' art at Paris's Salon d'Automne	•Birth of bandleader Cecil Scott	•Richard Strauss's opera Salome
6		•Death of Henrik Ibsen, Norwegian dramatist	•Birth of Shostakovich, Russian composer	•Schoenberg's First Chamber Symphony
7	•Janáček completes his opera Osud	•Picasso paints Les Demoiselles d'Avignon	•Death of Edvard Grieg, Norwegian composer	•Sibelius's Third Symphony
8	•Schoenberg's first atonal works	•Formation of the 'Ashcanners' artists	•Birth of Olivier Messiaen, French composer	•Mahler's Das Lied von der Erde
9	•First appearance of the Ballets Russes in Paris	•Italy's Futurist movement publishes its manifesto	•Birth of jazz musician Gil Rodin	•Webern's Six Orchestral Pieces, Op. 6
0	•Stravinsky's The Firebird premièred	•First abstract paintings by Wassily Kandinsky	•Birth of Art Tatum, American jazz pianist	•Alban Berg's String Quartet, Op. 3
1	•First performance of Der Rosenkavalier	•Birth of Elizabeth Bishop, American poet	•Death of Mahler	•Berlin's 'Alexander's Ragtime Band'
2	•Ravel's ballet Daphnis et Chloé premièred	•Death of August Strindberg, Swedish writer	•Birth of John Cage, American composer	•Schoenberg's melodrama Pierrot Lunaire
3	•Riot at Stravinsky's ballet The Rite of Spring	•First International Exhibition of Modern Art	•Birth of Benjamin Britten, British composer	•Debussy completes his ballet Jeux
4	•Opening of Berlin's Watch Your Step	•Publication of adventure story Tarzan of the Apes	•Birth of Billie Holiday, American blues singer	•Vaughan Williams's The Lark Ascending
5		•The Rainbow, novel by D.H. Lawrence published	•Birth of Frank Sinatra, American singer	•Debussy composes two sets of Etudes for piano
6	•Première of Strauss's Ariadne auf Naxos	•Monet paints series of Water Lilies	•Birth of Yehudi Menuhin, American violinist	•Nielsen's Fourth Symphony
7	•Original Dixieland Jazz Band's first recordings	•Dutch avant-garde artists publish magazine De Stijl	•George M. Cohan publishes 'Over There'	•Schoenberg sketches out oratorio Die Jakobsleiter
8	•Louis Armstrong plays with King Oliver's band	•Lytton Strachey publishes Eminent Victorians	•Birth of Leonard Bernstein, composer	•Stravinsky completes The Soldier's Tale
9		•Bauhaus school of art and architecture opens	•Birth of Margot Fonteyn, ballerina	•Richard Strauss completes Die Frau ohne Schatten

INDEX